918.66 Crespi, Jess.
CRE **Exploring Ecuador with the five themes of geography**

SOUTH RUTLAND
ELEMENTARY LIBRARY

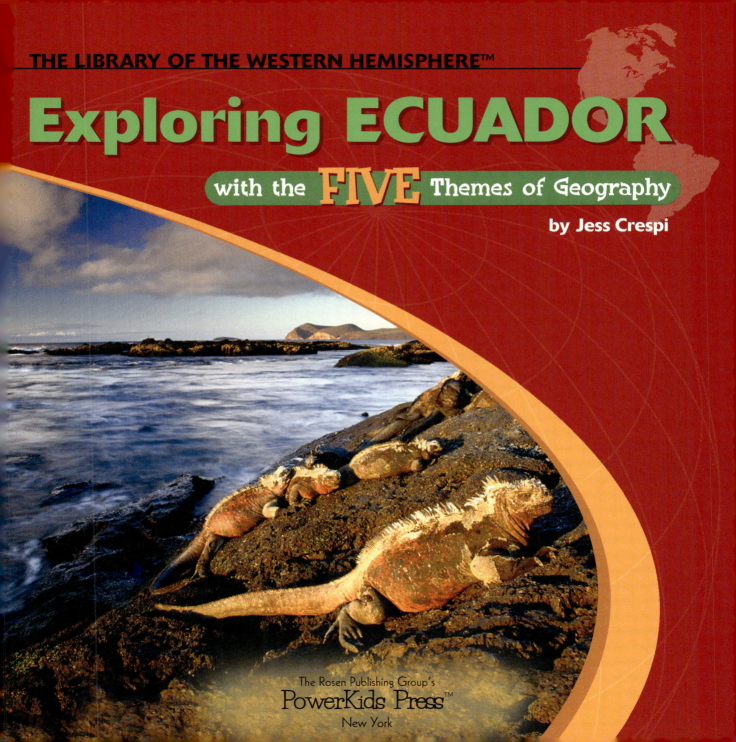

THE LIBRARY OF THE WESTERN HEMISPHERE™

Exploring ECUADOR

with the FIVE Themes of Geography

by Jess Crespi

The Rosen Publishing Group's
PowerKids Press™
New York

Published in 2005 by The Rosen Publishing Group, Inc.
29 East 21st Street, New York, NY 10010

Copyright © 2005 by The Rosen Publishing Group, Inc.

All rights reserved. No part of this book may be reproduced in any form without permission in writing from the publisher, except by a reviewer.

First Edition

Editor: Geeta Sobha
Book Design: Michelle Innes

Photo Credits: Cover, pp. 1, 10 © Art Wolfe/Getty Images; pp. 7, 9, 19 (Guayaquil), 21 © Pablo Corral Vega/Corbis; p. 9 (Rio Pastaza) © Alison Wright/Corbis; p. 10 (blue-footed booby) © John Giustina/Getty Images; p. 12 © Jeremy Horner/Getty Images; p. 15 © Grant Dixon/Lonely Planet Images; p. 15 (man with bananas) © Eric L. Wheater/Lonely Planet Images; p. 15 (banana export) © Owen Franken/Corbis; p. 16 © Medford Taylor/National Geographic Image Collection; p. 16 (Cayambe-Coca reserve) © Kevin Schafer/Corbis; p. 19 © Brent Winebrenner/Lonely Planet Images

Library of Congress Cataloging-in-Publication Data

Crespi, Jess.
    Exploring Ecuador with the five themes of geography / by Jess Crespi.— 1st ed.
    p. cm. — (Library of the Western Hemisphere)
    Includes index.
    ISBN 1-4042-2675-3 (lib. bdg.) — ISBN 0-8239-4635-5 (pbk.)
    1. Ecuador—Geography—Juvenile literature. I. Title. II. Series.

F3710.9.C74 2005
918.66—dc22

20040009

Manufactured in the United States of America

Contents

The Five Themes of Geography 4

1 Location 6

2 Place 8

3 Human-Environment Interaction 14

4 Movement 18

5 Regions 20

Fact Zone 22

Glossary 23

Index 24

Web Sites 24

The FIVE Themes of Geography

Geography is the study of Earth, including its physical features, resources, climate, and people. To study a particular country or area, geographers use the five themes of geography: location, place, human-environment interaction, movement, and regions. Each of these five themes helps us organize and understand important information about the geography of countries such as Ecuador. Let's explore and learn about Ecuador through the five themes of geography.

1 Location

Where is Ecuador?

To define where Ecuador is you can use its absolute, or exact, location. Absolute location tells exactly where a place is in the world. We use the imaginary lines of longitude and latitude to give a place its absolute location.

Relative, or general, location can also be used to locate Ecuador. Relative location describes where a place is in relation to other places near it. The cardinal directions of east, west, north, and south are also used when defining relative location.

2 Place

What is Ecuador like?

To answer this question, we must study the physical and human features of Ecuador. The physical features include landforms, natural resources, bodies of water, climate, and plant and animal life. The human features are things, such as cities, buildings, government, and traditions, that have been created by people.

3 Human-Environment Interaction

How do the people and the environment of Ecuador affect each other?

Human-environment interaction explains how the environment of Ecuador has affected the way its people live. It also explains how the people have adapted to the environment and how they have changed it.

4 Movement

How do people, goods, and ideas get from place to place in Ecuador?

This theme explains how people, goods, and ideas move around within Ecuador. It also shows how they move from Ecuador to other countries in the world.

5 Regions

What does Ecuador have in common with other places around the world? How are places within Ecuador grouped?

A region is made up of a group of places that share a common feature. This theme studies features that Ecuador shares with other areas, making it part of a certain region. It also looks at physical regions within Ecuador.

1 Location

Ecuador's absolute location is 2° south and 77° west. The relative location of Ecuador can be found by looking at the places next to it. Ecuador is bordered by Colombia to the north and Peru to the south and east. The Pacific Ocean borders the west coast of the country.

The Galápagos Islands belong to Ecuador. These islands are located in the Pacific Ocean, about 600 miles (966 kilometers) west of Ecuador.

Where in the World?

Absolute location is the point where the lines of longitude and latitude meet. Longitude tells a place's position in degrees east or west of the prime meridian, a line that runs through Greenwich, London. Latitude tells a place's position in degrees north or south of the equator, the imaginary line that goes around the middle of the earth.

2 Place

Physical Features

There are three different geographic areas on the mainland of Ecuador: the Costa, the Sierra, and the Oriente. The Costa is made up of coastal plains along the Pacific Ocean. The Sierra lies in the central part of Ecuador. It includes two mountain ranges, the Cordillera Occidental and the Cordillera Oriental, of the Andes Mountains. Between the ranges lie fertile plateaus and valleys. The Oriente, in the east of Ecuador, is part of the Amazon rain forest. It makes up about one-half of the country. The Galápagos Islands are 19 islands in the Pacific Ocean that are mostly made up of mountains.

Most of Ecuador experiences hot, humid weather. The temperature in the Costa is about 78°F (26°C). In the Oriente, temperatures can reach 100°F (30°C)

The Pastaza is a river that flows through the Oriente.

Cotopaxi is the world's highest active volcano. It is 19,347 feet (5,897 meters) high.

The land iguanas of the Galápagos Islands eat cactus, which provides enough water so that these lizards can go for one year without fresh water.

The blue-footed booby lives in colonies in the Galápagos Islands.

and there are about 80 inches (203 centimeters) of rain per year. The Sierra's temperatures are between 45° to 70°F (7° to 21°C), depending on the elevation.

Many rare animals, such as the tapir, the puma, and the endangered Andean condor, are found on Ecuador's mainland. There are also llamas, vicuñas, parrots, pelicans, crocodiles, snakes, and many types of monkeys. The Galápagos Islands are home to the giant turtle, the blue-footed booby, and the land iguana.

Forests cover almost one-third of Ecuador. Balsa and cinchona trees are found in the rain forests of the Oriente and the Costa. Mangrove trees grow along the coastal areas. The páramo is grassland that grows in the mountains. Certain types of cacti, cotton, and tomato can only be found on the Galápagos Islands.

The monastery of San Francisco, which was built in the 16th century, still stands in the city of Quito.

Quechua-speaking people live in the Andes Mountains areas.

Human Features

About 13,700,000 people live in Ecuador. More than half of the people live and work in the cities. Ecuador's government is a republic that is headed by a president. Most Ecuadorians are Native Americans or mestizos. Mestizos are descended from both Spanish and Native American peoples. Most other Ecuadorians are descendants of either Spanish settlers or Africans.

Ecuador's culture combines both Spanish and Native American influences. The official language of Ecuador is Spanish. However, many Native Americans and mestizos speak Quechua, the language of the Inca people who lived in the area before Spanish rule. Spanish colonial architecture can be seen in cities such as Quito and Cuenca. Music styles in Ecuador include the *yumbo*, *el sanjuanito*, and the *pasillo*.

3 Human-Environment Interaction

Most Ecuadorians live in the Costa area and the lowlands of the Sierra. Very few people live in the Oriente and the Galápagos Islands.

Ecuadorians rely on their country's wealth of resources. They get timber from the forests. The rivers are used to produce hydroelectric power. Fish such as tuna and shrimp can be found in the coastal waters. Mining for gold, silver, lead, zinc, and salt is essential to Ecuador's economy.

Ecuador's land is a valuable resource. Farmers grow bananas, coffee, potatoes, plantains, and sugarcane. Also, beef, pork, and dairy products are a large part of agriculture. Most farming is done in the Costa and Sierra areas.

Another important resource is oil, found in the northeast of the country. The Trans-Andean Pipeline was built to ship oil from the Oriente area, across the Andes, to the coast.

Bananas are one of the main crops grown in Ecuador, for both local use and for export.

The Trans-Andean Pipeline moves petroleum from the Oriente, through the Andes, to Esmeraldas.

Reserves such as Cayambe-Coca Reserve protect forestland from being cleared.

Ecuador is working to protect its mangrove forests in reserves such as the Mataje-Cayapas Mangrove Reserve.

The oil industry has affected Ecuador both positively and negatively. It has provided many jobs and resulted in the building of roads and housing. Unfortunately, in order to dig for oil, large areas of rain forests had to be cleared. Many Native Americans as well as wildlife living in these areas have had to move to other parts of the forests. The effects of pollution from oil spills on plant life and wildlife are also a large concern.

Ecuador's mangrove forest along the coast is also being threatened. These mangroves have helped to protect the land from the waves and winds of tropical storms. Many mangroves are being cut down in order to create shrimp farms in the water where the mangroves grew. In the northwestern region, almost all of the mangroves have been destroyed. The habitats of the animals that lived in the mangrove forests have also been destroyed.

4 Movement

Ecuador's transportation system is important to moving people and goods about the country. The roadway most used in Ecuador is the Pan-American Highway, a system of roads running through South America, Central America, and North America. Roads connecting cities and small towns are linked to the Pan-American Highway.

Ecuadorians travel along rivers, such as the Guayas and the Vinces, in boats and ferries. There are 205 airports in Ecuador. Both Quito and Guayaquil have international airports, and there are two small airports in the Galápagos Islands.

With about seven TV stations and over 300 radio stations, Ecuadorians all over the country can receive information. Several newspapers, such as *El Comercio*, *Ultimas Noticias*, and *El Universo*, are also sources of information.

Goods are shipped in and out of Ecuador through ports along the western coast. Guayaquil is Ecuador's chief port.

Ecuador has 26,841 miles (43,196km) of roadway. However, only 5,073 miles (8,164 km) are paved.

5 Regions

Ecuador is part of both cultural and geographic regions. It is part of a cultural region called Latin America, where most people speak a Romance language. Romance languages are Spanish, French, and Portuguese. Latin America is made up of countries in the Western Hemisphere, south of the United States, including the West Indies.

Ecuador is in the geographic region of South America. It is also a part of the region known as the Ring of Fire. This area borders the Pacific Ocean. Many earthquakes and volcanoes naturally occur in this region.

Geographic regions within Ecuador are the plains of the Costa, the mountainous Sierra, and the jungles of the Oriente. Ecuador is also divided into political regions. There are 22 provinces. Each province is divided into smaller regions, called cantons and parishes.

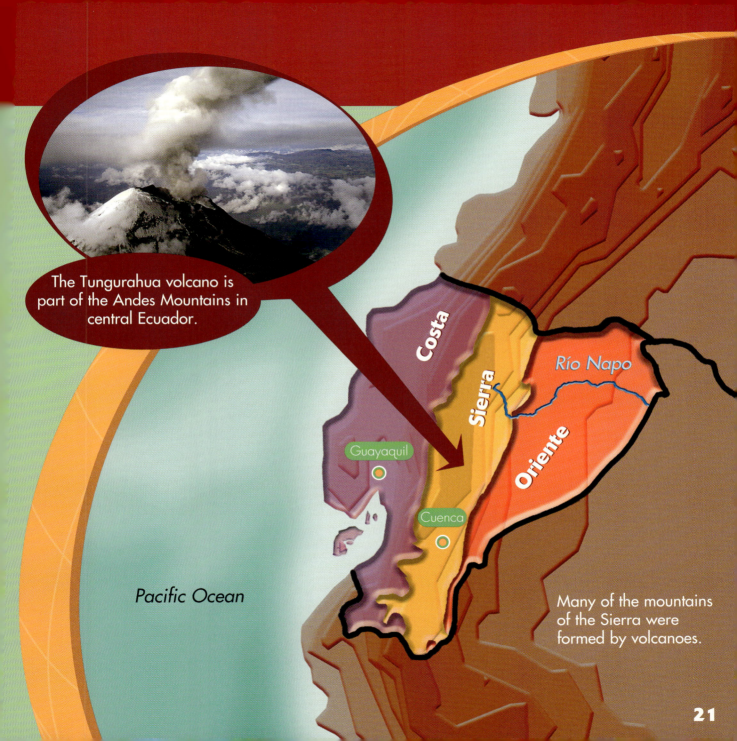

The Tungurahua volcano is part of the Andes Mountains in central Ecuador.

Many of the mountains of the Sierra were formed by volcanoes.

Ecuador's Flag

FACT ZONE

- **Population** (2003) 13,710,234
- **Language** Spanish
- **Absolute location** 2° south, 77° west
- **Capital city** Quito
- **Area** 105,037 square miles (272,045 square kilometers)
- **Highest point** Chimborazo 20,560 feet (6,267 meters)
- **Lowest point** Pacific coast zero feet
- **Land boundaries** Colombia and Peru
- **Natural resources** petroleum, fish, timber, and hydroelectric power
- **Agricultural products** bananas, coffee, cacao, rice, potatoes, manioc (tapioca), plantains, sugarcane, beef, pork, and dairy products
- **Major exports** petroleum, bananas, shrimp, coffee, cocoa, cut flowers, and fish
- **Major imports** machinery, industrial equipment, chemicals, raw materials, fuels, motor vehicles, and consumer goods

Glossary

descended (di-SEND-ud) To belong to a later generation of the same family.

endangered (en-DAYN-jurd) To be threatened.

fertile (FUR-tuhl) Able to grow plenty of plants.

humid (HYOO-mid) Damp and moist.

hydroelectric power (hye-droh-i-LEK-trik POU-ur) Electricity produced by water power that turns a generator.

interaction (in-tur-AK-shuhn) The action between people, groups, or things.

international (in-tur-NASH-uh-nuhl) Involving different countries.

plateau (pla-TOH) An area of high, flat land.

province (PROV-uhnss) A district or a region of some countries.

republic (re-PUHB-lik) A form of government in which the people have the power to elect representatives who manage the government.

resource (ri-SORSS) Something that is valuable or useful to a place or person.

tropical (TROP-uh-kuhl) To do with the hot, rainy area of the earth.

Index

A
agriculture, 14
Andes Mountains, 8
animals, 11, 17
architecture, 13

C
Colombia, 6
Cordillera Occidental, 8
Cordillera Oriental, 8
Costa, 8, 11, 14, 20

G
Galápagos Islands, 6, 8, 11, 18
Guayaquil, 18

H
habitats, 17

I
Inca, 13

L
Latin America, 20

M
mestizos, 13
mining, 14

O
oil, 14, 17
Oriente, 8, 11, 14, 20

P
Pacific Ocean, 6, 8, 20
Pan-American Highway, 18
Peru, 6
pollution, 17
province, 20

Q
Quechua, 13

R
rain forest, 8, 11, 17
region, 20
Ring of Fire, 20
rivers, 14, 18

S
Sierra, 8, 11, 14, 20
South America, 18, 20
Spanish rule, 13

T
temperature, 8, 11
Trans-Andean Pipeline, 14
transportation system, 18

Web Sites

Due to the changing nature of Internet links, PowerKids Press has developed an on-line list of Web sites related to the subject of this book. This site is updated regularly. Please use this link to access the list:
http://www.powerkidslinks.com/lwh/ecuador

**SOUTH RUTLAND
ELEMENTARY LIBRARY**